MW0041192 7

"The fact at the heart of S collection, *Imperative to Spare*, is stark. The beloved of some four decades, an ER physician in NYC, looks up at a 'bluebird sky' one year into the pandemic and drops dead. By turns poignantly honest and sardonically defiant, Hightower chronicles with rare brio the harrowing challenges of navigating the daily after his 'worst fear' has happened. How to go on? In these lucid, brave poems, Hightower shows us how. This necessary volume blazes a trail through despair to wisdom."

— Cynthia Hogue, author of *instead, it is dark*

"In a sequence of poems that moves us through cycles of profound grief, Scott Hightower mourns his long-term partner's sudden death. From deep shock to unshakeable sorrow, from re-emerging desire to the frank and sometimes funny self-assessment of his own aging and mortality, Hightower never fails to acknowledge that the experiences of love and loss are universal to the sentient being. 'What lies ahead lies ahead. Living things find/a drink of cool water soothing. Living things//like sleeping next to other living things.'"

— Kathy Fagan, author of *Bad Hobby*

"In his poem 'The Gaze,' Hightower writes of a man on the street: "I want // to lie down, / curl next to him / without perlustration, / without exchanging / a glace // or a word.' Fortunately for us readers, in *Imperative to Spare*, he has done quite the opposite: Hightower crafts a perlustration of grief that is unequivocally personal, profound, and with few peers. While his mastery of heightened language

remains clear, it's when Hightower's language arrives unadorned that we discern the total vulnerability of the poet in mourning: as in the middle of 'The World is Full of Beautiful Things,' where the speaker's gratitude for a beloved's absence is reminiscent of the great Russian poet Marina Tsvetaeva's plaintive utterances; or in 'Gashapon,' describing a candy vending machine, he writes, 'The sign reads: 'The light inside / is broken, but I still work.' // 'Me, too, vending machine. / Me, too…' Hightower's discrete moments with objects, memories of 'another set of eyes,' and a world unencumbered by his private pain elucidates the multivalence of a beloved's death. And all the little darlings—ourselves included—are better off knowing it."
—Daniel W. K. Lee, author of *Anatomy of Want*

"Even titans fall when their foundations are ripped from beneath them. In Imperative to Spare, the beauty of Hightower's intellectual expanse is bound in grief. He grapples with the pain of watching those further from the cause move ahead and faces grief as an active process— one we must participate in until finished (if it ever is). On the precipice of a perpetual trap door, he asks universal questions whose universality is the only comfort they bring. Who are we when love is lost? How do we rebuild? Is it worth it? Hightower doesn't have answers yet, but the quest has begun. Somehow, he stills finds moments to play. He sees himself in a vending machine, a wandering lamb, a perfume and marches onward with a torch to follow."
—Shelby Marne

IMPERATIVE

TO SPARE

Scott Hightower

REBEL SATORI PRESS
New Orleans & New York

Published in the United States of America by
Rebel Satori Press
www.rebelsatoripress.com

Copyright © 2023 by Scott Hightower
All rights reserved. Except for brief passages quoted in
newspaper, magazine, radio, television, or online reviews,
no part of this book may be reproduced in any form or any
means, electronic or mechanical, including photocopying,
recording, or information or retrieval system, without
the permission in writing from the publisher. Please do
not participate in or encourage piracy of copyrighted
materials in violation of the author's rights. Purchase
only authorized editions.

Book design: Sven Davisson

Paperback ISBN: 978-1-60864-292-2

Library of Congress Control Number: 2023946915

For Jóse

Jose Luis Fernández de Albornoz
(April 28, 1957 – January 30, 2021)

Acknowledgments

Grateful acknowledgements to the editors of the following publications, in which these poems first appeared, sometimes in earlier versions:

About Place Journal, Black Earth Institute, The Future of Water: "Ariadne Auf Naxos, With Her Regrets

Academy of American Poets, Poem A Day: "Last Privacy"

El Coloqui De Los Perros: "One Burning Candle"

Explorations: Don Yorty: "The World is Full of Beautiful Things"

RFD: "Empire Burlesque: Yet Again"

Tartessos: "At Aranuez," "At Las Castanueles in Aranjuez"

Contents

V. RENAISSANCE

"Con el tiempo todo pasa. He visto, con algo de paciencia, a lo inolvidable volverse olvido, y a lo imprescindible sobrar".

— Gabriel García Marquez

Eventually everything happens. I have seen, with some patience, the unforgettable become forgotten, and the imperative to spare.

I

Aubade Horribilis

Fate has parted us. I still live
diminished on the shore,
routinely visited with sunlight,

blue skies, incoming and outgoing
tides and waves. My days
once entrained the rising

and ebbing of shared rent,
sacrifice, and possibilities.
The bruises of frailties,

our victories, shared preferences.
Your dislike of tyrants
and raisins. Your choice

of republics, cities,
your freedoms. Your clean
open face. Your eyes.

The gentle wave of your hair.
Here, today, the cold surf—
last minion of the moon—

comes in and the hot
white of morning
morses heaven's blush.

Eau Du Bereavement: Letter That Seems To Want To Be A Poem

> "Why turning our life into an attention-
> whoring minstrel show of theatrical
> depression and misery probably isn't the
> best move"
>> —*The Big Book of On-Line Self-*
>> *Loathing*, an imagined book
>> featured in a meme on the internet

Sweetness,

I am fine. Thanks for your email. Like you,
in my dazzling sadness, I am bracing
for the widow's holiday gauntlet ahead.
I have declined all invitations by lying
to everyone, "I already have plans."
I don't, but being alone makes everything
so much easier. YOU know the feelings…
the drill. (Not that we don't enjoy a good party,

but no one seems to care for our brand
of last-year's perfume, "Eau du Bereavement."
(They do not know for ourselves alone,
we wear "Eau du Sorrow.")

What I want to know is if you are managing
new countenances? Whatever it takes, you
must hold to Joy. I will if you will. I know
what it is to be locked in a labyrinth
of tragedy... and solipsism. But trust me,
soon we will find our way out. Soon.

No Pain, No Gain: The Catalog

"The cure for pain is in the pain."

— Rumi

1972... Al Green was Austin's soundtrack.
Steeped in D.H. Lawrence

and "Women in Love," at a party,
I curled like a question mark,

groaned among coats and purses on
a bed. A friend, more mature,

far more in touch with the fluid
moment, sat and assured me

that the overspilling withdrawal
of the mirage of love almost throwing

me into a seizure was really

just the panic of a growing pain.

Less than a decade later, I held you
in my arms, a steady privacy

and companionable joy, every minute
with its price. On several continents,

we shared insights, deflected
judgments; earned our safe words:

dignity, full attention,
devotion and *freedom.*

Anechoic Venice

Through an open window, we
listen to someone play a violin.

The child trapped in our bodies
wonders, "Will I be held again?"

And the held one wonders,
"For how long?" In Venice,

through an open window, we
listen to someone play a violin.

The child trapped in our bodies
wonders "Will I be held again?"

And the one holding on
wonders, "For how long?"

From Here To There

"...a dream within a dream."
— Edgar Allan Poe

Somewhere over the rainbow
and in the dare that you have

the courage to truly lose
yourself in.... It's only a paper

moon. I would like to have someone
at the cemetery on the ranch

pull up the out of control,
decorative cypress (greedy thing—

it was suppose to be a dwarf!)
and replace it with a shoot

from the ancient pomegranate

planted at the corner of the old

house. Take care no one disturb
the miniature rose bush; it

will be faithfully blooming.
My present place is a block and a half

from the Madison Square Park corner
where the statue of Seward

(actually a portrait head
affixed to the elongated body

of Lincoln) sits. We—physician and poet;
happy, in our combined dreams come true—

frequently share burgers, fries, and half-and-half
iced tea and lemonades at the chiringito

there. The stately Empire State
Building towering in the distance.

It Would Have Been My Preference To Have Gone Before You

I don't have a clue
what to do
with me
as part of us
as a remainder.

This is… the antithesis
of Theseus's
operatic dream,

Ariadne's despair,
and my worst fear.

We Were Happy Here

"Wave of sorrow,
Take me there."
—Langston Hughes

To be brutally
thrown like boxes

back into the wilderness,
living without the eyes

of tenderness, without
Pandora's flutter,

evokes a little island
in the distance. Once,

a lonely islander turned to you.
Enthralled, you could have

drowned in his deep heart,
hope and sugar.

Gasping now.
Your only choices

are to sink, paddle,
or swim.

On My Own

Can one break promises
that were never spoken?
I wish we could do it all again.
This isn't how it was supposed

to end. I never dreamed
I would once again pilot
the onslaught of nights
on my own. (The suppositional

is the weakest of modes.)
But here I am, in pain
and wanting; time, living
in me. Now I am the one

who is passing. Rafting
alone isn't easy; covering
myself with the requisite
spells and incumbencies

of gratitude; the odd parallax
of death... and desuetude.
Resignation is the saddest virtue.
Much like returning to a familiar

landscape after a long trip
and not being able
to adjust one's frequency
to the native valences.

Long Hard Slog

"... the platonic amorist
of blue-breeched gondoliers..."
— Swinburne

A most trusted swamper—
indispensable, protective,
clear-eyed—hums, smiles, ties
and unties the raft at each banking,

while I study and fret over the ways
communities try to control their misfits.

My re-readings of Hawthorne's *The Scarlet Letter*,
Tennyson's *Idyll's of the King*,
and Kipling's *Stalky and Co*
(in the margin, did someone
really write, "they beat the fag"?)
proceed smoothly.

Hardy's *The Return of the Native*—
a slower read—was a precursor
to Andre Gide's *The Immoralist*
and Lawrence's *Lady Chatterley's Lover.*

Rosa Chacel's *Memoirs of Leticia Valle*,
and Nabokov's *Lolita*
both have roots in Tolstoy.

Animal Farm, *A Separate Peace*,
One Flew Over the Cuckoo's Nest,
The Bluest Eye await.

Mark's young man at the tomb, Eve
Adams, Langston Hughes, James Baldwin,
Rachel Humphrey's, and Tenika Watson
emerge as distinctive, inconvenient
presences, invasive species,
representations of "the weeds."

They don't elect to avoid us.

They want to eradicate us ... erase
us; wish... wash... us... away.

Old Dog

My beloved is either
hanging out

at a celestial ashtray
with a friend; or savoring

a preprandial
cocktail—a crystal

clear martini
with a lemon twist,

maybe a tarty sugar
or salt-rimmed margarita

or an aurora pink
cosmopolitan—

under a celestial
cork tree. We had

had all our shots.
Poised and measured,

I am a short-legged
dog in deep mud.

I don't know
how this shakes out.

Empire Burlesque: Yet Again

It's midnight. Another elegy? Really?
Another brutal salvage of love
wells and wants to come out?
I lost my buddy first; a lonely
penguin-masked polar bear
on a melting island of elegant ice.

And then, my brother. Nobody much
cared. Certainly neither light point
Presidents Reagan or Bush (the first one).

Later, when I attempted to enter
Bilie Jewel's biography onto
a Wikipedia platform
should a collector in the future
care to connect the painter to his narrative,
some unsung volunteer site deputy
dubbed my brother "a person
of insufficient consequence."

Pishkun, deep blood kettle,
buffalo jump. Ghost.

Then I wrote another for a celebrity
who wore lipstick, a talented
and oddly driven "company man"
with dyed hair, less nose than Tycho Brahe,
and an unsustainable Bob Fosse routine.
The stakes were high. Now, some of his
legacy is in lock-down, some adrift:
a catalog of music, some signature
moves, and three bestowed siblings.

Now here I am yet again writing
another; one for the love of my life.

One Burning Candle

Much like our Jacobeon Álvaro,
mushing issues of a new

constitution through ink
and practice; and Victoria Kent,

implementing the policies
of a precarious Second

Spanish Republic, it takes
a committed team; ahead

perhaps only faltering, losing—
even... exiled... for one's *side*.

"I'm not convinced it was
the wrong one," in custody,

Captain Reynolds
of the *Serenity* (a "firefly"),

responding point-blank
to Commander Harken.
"Geography may be
a bit difficult to arrange."

Tonight, we meet
Baltasar Garzón.

An arm-in-arm stroll through
Washington Square Park

brings us—film-makers,
physician, poet, judge—

to a table at Babbo. There
we discuss Ed Snowden.

Fellow pilgrim, the destinations
that draw us, drain us

of little virtue.
The starched cuffs

of your shirt remain
fresh-pressed

and crisp. The dignity
of international justice

is the grooming
of a kind of love.

At Aranjuez

In late Spring, one can eat *berenjenas de Almagro*—
pickled eggplant buds in Aranjuez. They are
deliciously messy; the juice drips down
one's chin. Once, I lived there in a house
with two front yards, each with its own
magnolia tree; one with a gurgling fountain
guarded by a ring of daisies and an owl,
the other with a table and chairs guarded
by a cloth edged with roosters. By the time
I lived there, the house was a luxurious
bungalow with a backyard bed of roses
and a swimming pool. Once it had been
a chicken coop with grounds and the simple
house of an earnest attending family.

When in Aranjuez, one is never far
from one of the rivers. Children carry real
and imaginary fishing poles. Two boys
paddle on the river; mischievous ones
attack the cane along its banks. Imaginary

Cleopatras take leave of their imaginary
Antonys, Laras take leave of their Zhivagos,
Constances take leave of their D'Artagnans,
Milady de Winter, of her long suffering Athos.
In town a boisterous social club for fishermen
and their cheerful families spills its
rambunctious music into the streets.

When one is in Aranjuez, one is never far
from one of the rivers. One is never far
from the imagination of power
or far from the power of imagination.
Sycamores line the lanes and curtain
the beautiful fields and orchards
and everywhere there is pollen in the air.

In Aranjuez, I removed a splinter
from the foot of a boy.

A LA CASA DE LA MONTA
Over the front door of the house I lived in
was a ceramic branch with two swallows,
their wings extended. Later, one of the men
who lived there took me to a house
he had lived in as a child. Over its great gates

in a peculiar curving cornice of stone
were two horses. Between them was a shield
with words inscribed. Latin:

Vento
Grabides
Ex Profile
Putabis

Parading around one's pedigree
is as capricious as playing with the wind.

At Las Castañuelas In Aranjuez

A small paddling of ducks
floats down, flutters

and feeds a bit.
The side of the palace

and the susurrating
cascade

is in afternoon shade.
As whole as I have ever
been any place
on earth: an afternoon

or a burnishing
"alpen" light

on the rustling
tree crowns above.
The little mutinous

armada without arms

works its way
up; down;

then, back
up again.

The World Is Full Of Beautiful Things

Over slippery stones
and through swirling streams,
he is my steady, soothing counsel.

He wouldn't have liked
growing into an aging
body. He is beautiful.
And today he dies.

He will never have to suffer
any disabling disease or illness,
or the corruptions of time.

He has it pretty good.
He has money in his pocket.
And my love. He will never have to grieve
losing me. This is Saturday.
A bluebird sky. He will not have to

be out Tuesday shoveling snow.
Designed to pass. Hang in there.
This morning, his day,
still intertwined. This day too,
will pass. His shadow.

He will not have to percolate decisions.
He will not have to seek peace beside
the still water. He will not have to endure

the stars in the sky. He will be thought.
He will not have to endure the kindness
of friends or strangers, the stares
of a city. He will not have to wait
for the scattering, even hope
for the shattering of new love.
He will not have to walk
through the days ahead
as if he owned them.

Shepherd's Song

(After Chants d'Auvergne, Baïlero
by Marie-Joseph Cantaloube)

Oh, now so much cleverness
on the other bank! If you find
my comely brother, he not only
plays the harp, but sings like an angel.

He and my other lovely friends will know
the best places to find shade and water
on hot afternoons. On dark nights,
I still use the little lamp you gave me.

They will know where to buy
small trinkets, creams, and the best
perfumes. I only knew you
on this side. You were the finest;

and, as I said before, cleverness
now abounds on the other side!

Song

Are you wandering
the hills of Úbeda
or are you coming home?

Little Bird, are you flying around
over the hills of Úbeda
or are you coming home?

Chirping Bunny, are you
coming home or wandering
the hills of Úbeda?

Kitten, are you
wandering the hills of Úbeda
or are you coming home?

Puppy, are you
coming home or wandering
in the hills of Úbeda?

Leaping Kid, are you
wandering the hills of Úbeda
or are you coming home?

Little Lamb, are you
coming home or wandering
the hills of Úbeda?

Lovely Calf, are you
wandering the hills of Úbeda
or are you coming home?

Little Colt with spindly legs,
are you coming home
or wandering the hills of Úbeda?

Are you coming home
or wandering
the hills of Úbeda?

Gashapon

Someone took a photograph
of a sign posted inside

a candy vending machine
window face.

As there is a slight reflection,
it is also a self-portraiture.

The sign reads: "The light inside
is broken, but I still work."

"Me, too, vending machine.
Me, too…." Now even as a bit

of an outlier, my inner compass
is fouled up… but my understanding

of my purpose and the dexterity
of my work remains clear,

acute, and intact. All poetry
is erotic. From someone's
mouth, to someone else's ear.

Last Privacy

Ancient kites, found in deserts
of the Middle East, are constructions

aimed at driving and trapping
game animals. They consist

of long dry stone walls
converging on a neck

which opens into a confined space
used as the killing floor.

The last night, unknowingly
I lovingly effervesced the long catalog

of my admirations for you into
your ear. Hammer strike

anvil. The last morning,
I studied you sitting

quietly studying the water
in the toilet bowl. I brushed

your hair. Gave you a kiss.
Told you, "I love you." Minutes later,

we walked outside our door the final time,
rode the elevator down together. Crossed

the lobby and vestibule, out the front door
onto the wide sidewalk of our building.

All the while, unaware of the drive.
Your last moments under a bluebird sky.

Your last moment standing
at the end of the fatal kite.

Estoque: Dance With Death

Call of the trumpet. In the center of the ring,
a red satin lined montera tossed
to the ground lands upside down
outside of our querencia. Pass
of the cape. No escape. No sidestep.
Volapié or *recibiendo*, the artery is cut.
You and your body slip away
forever. Embarkation. No destination.
Disembarkation. Amputation. Shadows.
I, a silk rosette, am left; slung across
endless ice with the wildness of love.
The dignity of the stadium grows dark.
No tenderness, no port.

I Do Not Exactly

I do often ideate the marigold /
saffron velvet scarf,

where we last lay his head.
The uninterrupted falling

of water on a friend,
gone in her shower.

A former roommate's wife gone
while sleeping on the couch.

I do not know exactly
what lies ahead for me.

I know, for now,
that sorrow chooses me.

It and snow are my only suitors.
I know that at the beginning

of each day, the ending of each
night, I choose the overflow

of solitude: stillness, private
restrained laughter, and song.

Imperative To Spare

Of course, I can point to the exact
spot. I was standing on the sidewalk
beside him at the curb. We exercised
our principles and judgments
happily six flights up. He routinely
kept the measure of the sun
and moon from our terrace,
had his final cigarette there.

I happily watched over him.
That morning I stepped
to the edge and I,
a bionic eye, am watching
him fall away
in slow motion.

Querencia

The house smells stale
and the bedroom ceiling
beneath the deck has
cracked and begun to leak.

The terrace above the street,
with its *sol y luna* vantage
of finality, has become
the *tendido* of the house,

just passing details of the nest
during this annus horribilis.

Expectations and uncertainty
of all that has been lost
gets addressed while running
the stained course
of each new day
in pinching *zapatillas*
and a suit of lights.

Continuing

I don't want the pipedream,
the perilous judgments
of nostalgia, the distortion

of the parallax. I don't want
a golden ticket to the valley
of candy with its river of chocolate.

I can deal with all the moving parts.
There's nothing anyone can "fix."
I'm trying to figure out

if I am still in a meaningful
conversation, what love means
beyond the amputation.

After Dickinson

Death came twice
(like Euridice
and Lazarus)

but I don't know
about its nailing
any eyes. It's true,

my life, now
beneath my feet,
is but an imitation

with little oil.
In my house, grief
is a no-warning

trap door
in the killing floor.

Cooling Board Blues

> Kneading on your lap is a cat's way
> of saying, "you're my person."

Like a phonograph's needle
skipping across vinyl grooves,
my concentration samples:
Some birds look very regal
in death. Under the sheet,
a ride on the glazing belt
can be lonely. A gentle

brush of the hair.
This is finality. Our farewell
moment. Good night, Sweet
Prince, my particular (only)—
never dismal—friend.
You have made it through
[needle skip]. Returning

to being a lone traveler

already feels almost
unbearable. A friend says,
"But that is love…."
(I am not so sure
that I need me,
but I still need you).

Enter Pain

In some situations, mourning
is another word for powerless.

There was never any clear inevitability
until the blow. Not knowing

what was actually happening
(obliged to occur) afforded shock.

Foresight be damned.
Later, finding the door ajar,

strapping pain—
having been delayed—

did not hesitate
to stride right in.

For Vasu

Laughter in the house.

Slaughter in the house.

Hard to get use

to living without

another set of eyes

Annus Horribilis

Shiva is used to sleeping
on a bed of uncertainty.

He blinks and a generation
has cut its teeth on grievance

and distilled resentment,
exhausted itself

with its screams
for retribution. More

than a passing bad patch
or a spell of misfortune:

a wounded planet
under a panicle of grief.

A lampoon
through the heart.

A harpoon
    through the harp.

Finally: amputation, you
ripped from me.

(Nail
that landing!),

a harpoon
through the heart.

Left Behind

I am a fucking ray of sunshine.
No tidy pop rom-com denouement
here. As far as I can tell, I daily engulf,
swarm, and overrun the airport of grief

like the doomed emergency departments
of hospitals in a covid spike
where some people (the anti-science,
hydroxichloroquine crowd) are now
taking a livestock de-wormer formulate
(ivermectin): apparently, anti-vaxer geeks
chasing and gulping down some irresponsible
entertainment's snake oil bark. Harm's way.

The ICU tipping point today is not
a bed and a ventilator. It is staff:
an amiable, well rested doctor or nurse,
a physical or respiratory therapist,
disciples of science. A staff:
a rough hewn knotty tree limb,

with a single snake coiling
around it. Good grief! I am
an ambulatory translator
caught in a story I can't walk out of.
No narrator. No narrative. No staff.

There is no visa renewal,
no retardant chemical drop
to quell the advancing fire
bursting across a granite ridge,

no capacity issue, no
convoy, no helicopter, no airlift,
no evacuation for me.

"A sunbeam, a sunbeam,
Jesus wants me for a sunbeam...."

FIRE MOVEMENT
Here there is no compassion:
no purity, no morality, no truth.

(Not even a snake.)

Just heat, glowing embers, and smoke.

MORE LIKELY TO STAY BEHIND THAN LEAVE
August thirtieth, 2021, as the last
U.S. troops exited Afghanistan,
at least 5o dogs were believed
to have been left behind.

Once, not long after telling me
he was on path to becoming a physician,
that he wanted to ride a donkey
up to Santorini, to cruise up the Nile,
and to raft the Colorado,

Jose told me he wanted me
to be his exclusive traveling
companion, wanted me devoted
only to him, "Someone to have
my back. You're *the guy
one wants to ride the river with*."

I wanted him to see the Ganges.

The strength of the bond between U.S.
military service animals and their handlers
made the spokesperson skeptical that
handlers would abandon their partners.
"They'd be more likely to stay behind
than leave without them."

With the situation unraveling, crates
of dogs had to be released into the airport

turning once-rescued shelter dogs
into homeless strays." No
tidy pop rom-com denouement.

Denouement As Nataraja

In his right hand: Damaru,
the drum that makes

the first sound of creation.
Agni in the other, all powerful

flame, sacred ash. Death
capable of knocking out

two rivers, two birds,
two dancers, a couple —

with one heart attack;
two deaths, only one discard.

The expression of his lower
right hand makes abhaya mudra;

(not compassion, but the intimation
that allays fear). Sanctum. Shelter.

Humbly take the dancing warrior's sooth.
Ode of gestures. Ode of gaze. Bhajan.

Shiva's front left hand, indicates
his raised left foot, Charan Sparsh.

Praise, the bend of gratitude, balm,
relief from pain, refuge for troubled

frailties. Shiva's supporting right foot
tramples the pipe dream of deceptive

illusion; charm, no enchantment.
Let no dreams—the transports

of transparent horn— blandish
or adorn the silent house of Sleep.

Artful ivory gate. Back to earth
wind, water, dimension, and fire.

Interchangeable garments,
measure—linear/cyclical *

historic/mythic * (heroic/divine);

measure—outside of time.

The Widow Scarlett

> "Let the beauty you love,
> be what you do." — Rumi

Tugboats. Small, tough,
determined, happy vessels
moving large, lumbering ships
to their proper places.

Rather like teaching, perhaps.

Sooner or later, we all
must recognize the limits
of our expenditures,
find alternatives.

Hyper capitalism can be
a tragic embarrassment
to an empathetic and honorable
decency.
              It's possible, too,

that a very-tight-knit-family member
may choose a mate who they know,
on some level, will not blend
or buy into family expectations.
That happens, where one
may want some distance,
boundaries. Thus they seek out
marital reinforcements.

This is not exactly what was
planned; but here I am,
a pile of ravenous embers
on the beach…. Who once lived
with another set of eyes. Found pleasure
in dependably putting a smile on
someone else's face. To have
been petted. To have petted.
The innocent feel that they
will live forever. The old,

themselves embers,
know they will not.

Less from the flaming gem—
more artifact, these lays drift

from a bonfire on the beach
down from the tower

of confinement, reify
from the germ
of favor and sorrow.

Forebear The Poisonous Suitor

Pain and missing are more than
just phenomenological ideation,
are a traumatizing disruption.

Parched space. How does one go on?
The new harsh insistency most
likely—more often than threat—

is undesired encroachment.
It arrogantly looms, proffers
to be, itself, the new

heartless organization.
If one is to go on, it, indeed,
will have to be accommodated.

Accept. Accommodate where one can,
but continue to judiciously eye
the coldly assigned and assumed.

Just because one is parched
does not mean one need
drink poison. Except. Forebear.
Resolve not to yield those
moorings nutritious and vital
to your self-possession.

III

Vanities

(*Samson and Delilah*, Peter Paul Rubens, ca. 1609/10, Collection of the National Gallery, London, probably a fake)

The profile of the crone
with a candle echoes
Delilah's. Delilah's light
auburn European hair

curls down the far side
of her neck, down to him.
Her pale-pink left hand
oddly remains tenderly

melted on Samson's back.
May there still be faintly
a whisper there: "It is
a privilege to be included

in your privacy." All that
well lit hunk and weight
of muscle has finally collapsed
into its own tan ocean of lust;

slips and floats in the dream
of Delilah's rustling Philistine rose
and copper finery, germ of deception
and betrayal. One of his hands—

tenderly grasping—pillows
one of his cheeks. "Lambs, and all."
The near intimacy of the lovers
is almost locked, and timeless

in its allowance of the enterprising
cluster of others. They team.
Snip. Snip. Where are the toes
of his foot? Outside

the open door,
atmospherically lit,

her conniving, armored
associates await.

Spleen

"La plus belle des ruses du diable
est de vous persuader qu'il n'existe pas."
— Charles Baudelaire, *Paris Spleen*

For years I was diligent about keeping
Cerberus turned away (… that creature
came to really hate me) "a saint

to madness or a king to his knees."
I long served as sentinel by the door,
the dependable boundary

between you and the tenacity
of family judgment and mischief.
Deep as my affections were,

their valence
was not just macroscopic.
I could not protect you

71

from the exquisite,
from the invisible deadly,
from what you—from childhood—

were taught was trustworthy.
Try as I might, I grew to understand
that I could not protect you

from a forced wrong
transplanted
into someone else.

View From The Ditch

It's nice to have dominion over
serpents and scorpions, to live

with another set of eyes; to trust
"Nothing by any means shall hurt you,"

life's possibilities and mysteries,
to be petted and to pet.

Jesus in *Luke*: "Who is my neighbor?"
And before that, *Leviticus:*
"How shall the stranger be treated?"

The sojourner fallen among thieves.
The man in pain. Empathetically,
the Samartian's view reaches toward

 the man in pain, the view from the bottom

of the ditch where the dog shits.)
Why flaunt your good blessings?

Why bother to cast dispersions
on those whose wings are clipped,
no fault of their own?

Twice passed by,
on the other side …
"rock bottom" surmised

as being a kind of self-indulgence.
The Samaritan goes to he fallen
sojourner and bestows him

mercy. What's mine is yours,
if you have need of it. My safety
is yours, if you have need of it.

The Gaze

A cool early evening,
I am managing
my burdens home.
Along the way,
I can smell the man's

stench before I see
him on the grate
looking up
at me. Oddly,
I want

to lie down,
curl next to him
without perlustration,
without exchanging
a glance

or a word;
I want

to lie down,
tuck into him,
and rest.

Empty Hands

Territorial aggression, myopia, combativeness,
disruption, weaponizing, and torturing others
out of a notion of perfectionism are not new
conditions. They are just shifting risk factors.
Another week of teaching, and then I'm free.

Observations, responsibilities, freedom.
I took off the final load of his clothes today.
I was heading to the local thrift store,
but my gaze caught a young immigrant vendor
selling garments on the sidewalk. Thinking,

Hell, if you're putting them out there
for capitalism, this is capitalism
at its rawest, I offered the bags to her
instead. She seemed baffled. These days,
boundaries are a very fluid game.

In practicing the art of floating social
engagement, one moves with extreme

sensitivity to the shifting terrain. It both
sustains... and exhausts. When the going
is smooth, be grateful. When the going
is rough, attempt to be graceful.
She was very concerned about what I—
standing there with empty hands—expected
in return. What more was there for me
to do but to turn and walk away.

Hanging From A Rose's Stem

"I can hear the almost unhearable sound of the roses singing." — Mary Oliver

Move over Ms. Oliver, I can hear
the unbearable song of the roses.

My friend, Barbara, a "real" Texan born,
horse-riding pistol, poetry toting gal,
who learned "to watch out for the stinger,"
and heard Ethel Merman sing the paean
"Everything's coming up Roses"
in Chicago when she was twelve,

can hear the sound of the rosé
singing, "Well there's a rose
in the fisted glove. And the eagle
flies with the dove." Hear the umbrella?
Life's possibilities and mysteries?

… une fleur unique au monde,
qui n'existe nulle parte,
sauf dans ma planéte....
 Ever see the old Science fiction
movie "The Fantastic Voyage"?

I also know a joke about a patient
who had a crush on his proctologist?
(I hear the word is now antique,
that we are supposed to say "colorectal
surgeon"). When he was in for his examination,
the doctor said, "I feel something irregular.
I'm going to have to penetrate a little deeper.
Yes… Yes… There is something....
My lord, son, you have a dozen
red roses crammed up inside of you!"

The patient coyly replied, "Read
the card, Silly. They're for you."

Just A Country Boy

 Yep. The shame is the way that life
just kept its foot on my neck. I've never
really done much besides write…
travel, and care for those I've loved,

taught young critters and tended
growing plants. "When a plant doesn't
thrive, you have to adjust the environment
it grows in, not the plant." Oh,

and I've done a little scrubbing and cooking
along the way. Many found my country
humor akilter. I know some about life's
possibilities. Nothing much about

its mysteries. My vocabulary and notions
are both simply received, not what's
at stake. As for my prayers (the stuff
that just moves forward): just something

I said in private. As for my song
(the stuff that turns back on itself):
just what I wrote down, just something
to hear ... maybe something to read.

Dude, Don't Cut Off Your Feet!

"Don't cut off your iambs." Red Shoes.
Cow patties! Prosodic measure. Truncated
canvases and unmindful photo framing.

Sampson's hair…. (It's all perspective
and process, isn't it?) Good Lord,
the toes of one of his feet!

Cutting off your feet
to get out of shackles
may not be a very good plan.

However, gnawing off your feet
to get out of a lethal trap
might well be a realistic strategy.

Sampson At The Mill

THE MUSEUM OF ALONENESS

Legally, the probate should be closed out,
the estate tax payment made. I have met

with lawyers, bankers, accountants,
translators, notaries, consulate assistants.
And then there is The Unhelpful
Hurricane that cannot Help Herself.
This probate is grinding me down.

It's been too many months.
I am beginning to feel
like Regina Lampert, a painful
beauty, "We are in a moment
and a reckoning. Tara,
Tara, all are true at once;"

or, in another tricky moment.
"Do you mind if I smoke?"

"I wish you wouldn't."
I've gone from "Summer of 42"
to "The Single Man"... a little "Harold
and Maude" thrown in for seasoning.
It's not easy being a painting
on the wall of a mine that's caving in,
Sampson grinding at the Philistine mill.

With covid, the consulates
and courts are slow as molasses.

A friend shares a quote with me,
something a character played by Jane Russell
said to a character played by Robert Mitchum:

"Everybody's lonely and worried and sorry.
Everybody's looking for something."

When I worked on the ranch,
my Dutch grandfather talked with me
about "coming up on another man's work,"
recognizing what another had done,
the improvements others had made

before you.
                    He taught me
          to finish my work.
And then to go back and look at it again
minding that one day another might
come along and study what I had done,
before they began to build on it.

He taught me to go back and do any—
even the smallest things I might identify—
to be sure the job, my job, was

finished. (That is where I learned
to put "finish" on a poem.)

He outlived my grandmother.
He died… a heart attack at the back
garden gate going out to do chores,
an empty pail in his hand. Speck
was as at his side, still
with him when we found him.

You are in a bit of a bad patch, but you

will come out of it on the other side;
and, this ordeal will pass. Perhaps more
accurately, you will pass through
this ordeal. You have the gift
that the end of this present experience
will soon be in sight. Trust me. To be
in a bad patch with no end in sight
is altogether something else.

CARL HEINRICH BLOCH'S "SAMSON IN THE TREADMILL"

The beginning of what will eventually
be finished by David. A judge.
A man in pain; blinded…
and in pain… who, in spells,
conveniently surrenders himself
(lambs and all) because he
is weak and emotionally frail,
no matter how strong he appears
in the eyes of the public.

My Iron Mask

In all recent photographs,
exquisite sadness,
cruel and exceedingly brutal,
seems to be a new indelible
detail in my eyes,
even when I
am smiling, content,
thinking of you.

IV

The Damned Probate

The damned probate is like beavers
in a river. There is a log jam.
You move a stick. Things give a little.
You keep going till the thing
gives way... and the water
runs free.... And then a little later,
down the river, you come to...
another dam. Rinse, Repeat.
Dream about not studying
for the test, sitting
in a desk at school
and not being dressed,
wake up,
and your worst dream
is that you are not dreaming...
and that you have to go to work
on the damned probate.

Dream

"Wash the plate not because it is dirty nor because
you are told to wash it, but because you love the
person who will use it next."

— St. Teresa of Calcutta

Come, I will take you
out into the reeds
where we can be
together, talk (...or not),

raise our eyes, take in
the old ivory moon;
leave our waste,
make our water.

Here, you may feel hope
gently rocking away
from where the tongues
of the world clatter.

On the outside,
you can still yourself;
and, on the inside,
feel it lapping.

My belovéd died in the center
of a city that he loved.
On the Manhattan sidewalk
where he drew his last breath,

where we laid him down,
was spray stenciled:
DREAM UNTIL
IT'S YOUR REALITY

Feet To The Fire

"To a snail, a duck is a vengeful god."
—Nancy Holder

Like a cat ever bringing
a mouse home to you,
I had to become highly

compartmentalized,
judicious, and discrete.
We are not designed to last.

Each is but passing through.
The world is large, and in a larger
vastness of desire lines.

You and I coursed through
in a measured pattern of days.
Our currency was the current knowledge

of the world, be it clinical disease protocols
or poetry—oddly limited, oddly finite:
always with an eye to the determination

of final form. I have heard it said
that the tiny is the last refuge
of the tremendous.

Ariadne Auf Naxos, With Her Regrets

(*Rest on the Flight to Egypt*,
Luc Olivier Merson, 1879)

I have given up on both: my mother's
Dignity and my father's religion;
Floating, arms and legs out, face down…
I prefer the beauty and terror of the lessons

Of a remote lagoon. I am diminished,
Abandoned, and as melancholic as
That painting that will follow: a weary
Young mother fleeing with her newborn.

The baby glowing like the radium face
Of a spectral watch; the two of them,
Dredged in desert dust, cradled in the paws
Of an ancient sphinx. She is beautiful

And barefoot; the night is chilly, clear, blue.
What lies ahead lies ahead. Living things find
A drink of cool water soothing. Living things

Like sleeping next to other living things.

Warm Bodies

I want to get to a day where I am
doing more than surviving.

I can do "cute." I can pull off "nice."
I have even had some use

for "mean." It's mine, all mine.
Not so much "cut adrift"

as immersed and consumed,
at the same time. Bewildered.

Between now and then,
it's crunch time.

I'm just endlessly burning,
"enduring" each day.

I don't wish this sort
of existence, or deal,

on anyone: warm
bodies worrying

about me on thin ice,
a tragedy

that seems destined
to inevitably flow

into the sea,
eventually to be

a wave
becoming the sea,

to be a wave
becoming the sea.

Herding Lawyers Is Like Herding Cats

An old idea
whose moment may have come....

After herding lambs all day,
at the end of the day,
all the little darlings were castrated.

Asking For A Friend

Can I classify making a firm date
in the teeth of a singles ap
as a nosocomial alternative
to Switzerland? When
does one roll the dice? Who
will take notice of me making
an appointment with an astrologist?
Residual systems? Incomplete?
Unfinished? Artful. Imperative?
Spare? Much of the world
is a modified re-creation
or a brand-new creation every day.

Grief As Improvisation

"How do you eat an elephant?
"One bite at a time!"

Death is the cue, the prompt, "the elbow."

Hard to hold out your hand
when Death has already bitten
both of yours off.
Hard, when you feel clumsy
as if small bunches of branches
have been jammed into the ends
of each of your arms.

"Carry on!"

Love is the habituating
elephant in the room,
not Death.

Despair is The Mud Wrestling Pig.
Pass the bait....

You know what will happen
if you don't resist it....
Everybody will get dirty.

 This is your rodeo!

Keep going. Keep singing.
Don't worry about who hears
or what they think.
Mind yourself
as best you can.

Take care to give
from the overspill,
not the well. For now,
just ladel out what you can.

Hold up your head:

"Yes, and...."

When Your Can See It All As Inevitable Process

I have always migrated to people
who take care of plants, animals,
children, or physically cared

for other people; artists
who observe, make things, draw,
record, appropriate the body

Unable to find a way out, I ceaselessly
cast about, living in my own state
of unevenly bleached out, laughing
at the reflection of glimmer on water.

Inevitable: the determination
of formal elements—be it
"the law," "the period,"

or "the grave." "Really, Lord,

will you ask me to clean,
repair, and rebuild again?"

The kingdom of Heaven
is no spiritual roof-garden
or palisade: it's inside you.

And so I
start rebuilding
again.

My Pandemic

"Nobody else can be alive for you."

My mirror reflects the expression
of a predicament, a single man:
my pandemic. my quarantine.

Back in the saddle.
Just get through the day.

*

To everyone who comes into my
physical or virtual path, I
am existing in a perpetual state
of bewilderment… which, turns out,
is good for my practice poetry…

but not so good for inter-personal,
public, private relationships,

not so good for generally
moving though the world.

I've ruffled some feathers.
A shrug. A lamb's nap.
My pandemic.

Holding something in each hand
and going up stairs, one must balance,
take to the middle of the treads.

Posse, neighbors, and mourners,
toggle of justice, score settlers.
Depends on ethos: good guys,
or a swarm of dangerous
vigilantes or greedy predators.

Poor sweet thing, Euridice. I can't tell

if she is thriving or dying. One
of her leaves looks beyond return.

The slow as molasses probate inches

forward and grinds me down
at the same time. Terrace patched.
Deck restoration scheduled for tomorrow.

My new roommates are two potted
refugee plants. They are
terrific companions. I think
they're happy, but they drink a bit.

And then to discern and consider
the days behind, ahead; sift,
rifle through the stars.

To contemplate: to lay out
a plan in a specific landscape,
a castle in the air, to again be
a scorpion navigating by the stars.
They have but three to fifteen years.

"*Everyone* parts with *everything
eventually*, my dear" (—Time).

My great-grandmother's
house in central Texas
had magisterial front steps

leading up to the front door.

Corinthian column caps edged
the majestic wrap-around porch.
Its ceiling was painted haint;
a swing at one end,

a set of porch-broad stairs
at the other.

Snowman On The Terrace

The idea of magical underwear has its appeal.
"A bit Quixote. Way too Giacometti.
More generosity... then twig jazz hands!"
Blessed are those who can reach,
eventually grasping onto a bit
of hope beyond despair.
Santeria swami with rainbow
beads around his neck!

I have been thrown, encountered
"the worst fear," and survived.

Unable to find a way out, I ceaselessly
cast about, living in my own state
of unevenly bleached out,
laughing at the glimmer on water.

At least once I had the courage
to lose myself in something
I truly wanted, shamelessly

ran the risk of being the one left
holding the cards. What goes
into the heart stays in the heart.

Candles, a pack of cigarettes
and a cosmic cocktail, a martini…

(Damn the carcinogenic and poisonous.
"If you have to walk through hell,
walk as if you owned the place!")

… a whole bottle of vodka!
A pandemic snowman needs
his post-prandial dry and chilled.

Now, to just worship it… until it melts.

Lone Bird On The Water

No drama. Some lonely, foolish
sentimental moments. Some poised,
some not so poised; but all on track.
Be it the first of many more
adventures or one of the last...
be it one of the good ones. With you,
even the dismal was beautiful.

Self-Worth, No Rights Reserved

Thank you. "For what, Sir?" For
your time, your counsel, your eyes.
For your gaze reflecting whatever
it is we are passing through.

You are no mere "font of thin advice."
You are measured perspective, a gesture
of kindness, compassion, and trust.
I am a fellow traveler, a sojourner.

A strong drawbridge offers a night
respite. a chance at a retreat, needed
rest, or repair (or brings distant
dangers in striking range).

I would happily lay my head down
beside yours on a pillow made
of a vista of the gracefully turning
necks of horses or a clean cold creek.

As for me, my bread is on the water.
I am a merry widow catalog
of cliches. They say Fortune
favors the bold. It will either raise

me up again or take me down.
"Riding the wave all the way…!
I am yours, and you are mine. Sir,
I know I can call on you if I need you.

Acknowledgement

Please, no cheers (No
Clowns!). No advice,

or lunging ahead or
away. No trying to fix it.

No distraction or wreckless,
knee-jerk projects.

No attempting
to make things better.

Simple dishes
of comfort welcomed.

Just your company.
Just being heard

makes things better,
even when they can't be

made right. Thank you
for your support.

Thank you for listening.

Besos Enormes

"If it's going to be a world with no time
for sentiment, it's not a world that I
want to live in."
— Christopher Isherwood, *A Single Man*

You can grow anything
anywhere, if you know

how to, if you are
willing to care for it.

It feels good to have
someone calm and solid

fiddle with your hair.
Bring on the potted plants,

a pet, love rented
by the hour, I'll grit

my teeth…. One more
gaudy night! More makeup,

less bacon, one less
set of season tickets,

more jewelry—"but what
a way to be cheapened;"

one more dip, last
milking, more time

to write! I have been
making pasta sauce,

and chili, for years.
Have always chopped

the onion. ("Cutting
a bitch" is in the recipe.

Fuck around with
me and find out)

Silly me, a cooling

ray of sunshine,

I have survived
my worst fear.

I've watched
all of mine pass.

Been there to ease them
into their transition.

I anticipate panting
like an old cow

to my own death,
no one else's.

The bomb gone off
on the inside,

body burned,
ashes disposed of—

I want my passage
to take me

to becoming either
a short-horned lizard

or a bottle tree.

Rosa del verano

La rosa exquisita del verano,
no destinado a quedarse por diseño,
sigue siendo una delicadeza
de gran belleza.

Rose Of Summer

The exquisite rose of summer,
not made to last by design,
is yet a delicate thing
of great beauty.

Empty Arms

Unlike the pressed flower
or lock of hair, the bones,
the stone, the stenciled dates,
or the traced shadow. Language
and the reality parallel to it
is all we've really got.
Imaginative signification
makes for discomfort:

the number, the spoken word,
the written word, the sentence, the sketch,
the painting, the photograph, the bones,
the snowman, the idol, the monument,
the overly sentimentalized, romanticized
reiterations of the beloved, the random
memorabilia, unnatural
commemorations, the pipe dreams.

This spring, I will have roses, coleus,
and sweet potato vines; basil and mint;

and side boxes of soft pink geraniums,
trimmed with yellow and an edge
of a small purple flower that you loved
but whose name I can never remember.

Small Monument

A stone sculpture stands in the garden
where both some grapes of wrath

and some seeds of peace and abundance
are stored. No souped-up device

amplifies my transmission
of frailty, guidance, or hope.

No one kisses my lips.
No one brings me offering

or sacrifice. My victories
and defeats are all accounted for.

V. RENAISSANCE

Meditation: Point Of The Eyes

Stillness and the discomfort gap
and the distributor cap.

"Do you enjoy the way
I clean a plate?"

"Who will fill
my absence?"

You are afraid
of me. Of my surety of principles

and my frailties.
Though you lead

and I but serve.
The work of attempting

to look the abyss in the eye
and not blink goes on.

Oh how we
take one day at a time,

one night at a time;
count the kittens,

smell and enjoy
the puppies.

Urgencies: no shame,
No secrecies.

Baby, who else holds time,
is offering you the world?

Resourceful people
bring a lot to the table:

Myrtle Beach, a bungalow
in Poona, a penthouse terrace

in Manhattan.
Comfort, peace,

and respite from pain.

A blunt.

You and your
abrupt endings.

You with your bag,
me with my pillow.

                  Me, and mine.

You are safe with me.
We all have to learn to live

with the detectable
and the undetectable,

the treatable and untreatable
disorder. I can't quit you

any more than I can control
the earth and the sun,

the clock, attached,
unattached,

detached,

the treatable
and untreatable order.

Why does anyone die?
Like abrupt exits,

I am used to disapproving,
even resentful eyes.

Not yet used to trusting
your morsing eyes.

The work goes on.
Guide me. Teach me.

Discovery Waltz

After Cavafy's "Ithaca"

Discovering that there is some loneliness
and misery in your journey,

your escapades, that along the way
you are going to have to do
with some placeholders

in the place of some real things
you would much prefer,

does not in any way mean
that Truth, Beauty, and Goodness
have failed you. It just means

you—a wily, poetic traveler,
a survivor—are chafing against time,

permission, fashion; that you are attached
to comforts that you have lost.
Loneliness and misery are not meager

chains. They, too, are but truths
that can avail themselves to you.

Faiths. The promises of hope and love
they elicit in the distance are not mirages.
They are not the new. They, too,

are original. They, too, are accesses
to a bounty for which you have begun

to pine: a new poem, a new blue
couch; a clean, clear new spring;
a bounty waiting for you.

Whazup * Intact * Fine And Dandy

"Ever has it been that love
knows not its own depth
until the hour of separation."
— Kahlil Gibran

Unfortunately, some of us know
what it is to have one's life crash like a plane,
to be a glass vessel of grief entirely filled
with fire, thrown into a new
secular, transactional world:
"Dollar Pizza," "A dollar fifty for pool,"
"More than twenty will get you more attention."

I started with "A Single Man," "Harold
and Maud" and "Summer of 42." I feel a bit

like a sage wandering along in the underworld,
at times, like a character in "Cabaret"
or "Rent" …. or maybe even "The Blue Angel."
Do you know Gus Van Zant's "Mala Noche"?
 (Damned autocorrect) keeps wanting
to make it "Male Note."

I serendipitously met
and bonded a bit
with a kid.
              I was widowed by a heart attack
at 68. He was widowed by violence at 25.

One night a week he works near my place
as a barback. He gives papís lap dances
for money a couple of nights a week.

Some nights he comes to my place, I buzz
him in and he crawls into my bed.
We never touch one another.

He busts a nut, beds down a kid… and tells me

all about it. He messages me
and comes by every few days.
On the phone, we sign off with "I love you."
It is a very odd furrow that lad and I are walking.

"People are just as wonderful as sunsets
if you let them be. When I look at a sunset,
I don't find myself saying, 'Soften the orange
a bit on the right-hand corner.'
I don't try to control a sunset. I watch
with awe as it unfolds."

Drag queens reveal a notion of femininity
like Machisto cowboys reveal a notion
of masculinity. Neither is about being immature
or mean spirited. *That* is the estate of Hate.

Detach from what one can.
Care for what one must.

One can grow something—organs,
antlers, velvet—almost anywhere
if one understands the rules of engagement

and the principles of specific care.

"Whatever you want.
I can make you happy."

Just a kid I know, a young man,
a lamb. I knew another lamb.

Shall we take in some version of the Greek tragedy
Orpheus and Eurydice, Puccini's *La Bohéme*,
Verdi's *La Traviata*, some version
of *The Lady of the Camellias* (Charles
Ludlam's *Camille?*), *Moulin Rouge?*

Everyone so anxious! The young,
so full of misgivings and hope,
the uncertainty of achievement.
The old, so full of past.
Trivial encounters of daily
existence are in the end
what most of life is. Was
not my case. My days of building
were full of extraordinary people,

adventure and travel, amazing
places retted by history,
a chorus of lovely languages
and shelves full of great books.

About the woodlands I will go
To see the cherry hung with snow.

That we care so much leads to our despair.
The attachment of hope leads to despair.
Leads to constant repair:
entitlement, victimhood.

Aimless? Abandoned? Hurt? Lost
everything that meant something to you?
Emptier than the sound of your own echo?

Learn to worry less about what lasts,
about what things cost. *Every* moment
is just a fragile bubble. Look

to the skies: resistant
to worthless obedience;
obedient only to the universe.

Resilience, fuel, scarcity,
cold, fire, interaction;

Eternity: majesty, sanctity, sanctuary.

Urgent Care

URGENT CARE - 1

Here, my state radiates out
to (from) where some manifestation
of the uniqueness of my trauma
and my practice of reminding (writing)
collide.

                         Illusive balance:
beyond the banal and the bureaucratic
to the cartesian and the transcendental.

Backdrops /landscapes of ongoing disaster
and survival:

      New York City, New Orleans.
      Detroit, Uvalde, Maui, Fill in the Blank
      with lots of places in our country, our world.
      Fill in the Blank with Your Name here.

Why mix in your family?

Why mix in Jefferson writing his drafts
of the Declaration of Independence,
the U.S. Constitutional Convention of 1787,
or Alvaro de Albornoz Liminiana, the first
President of the Spanish Constitutional Court of
                    Guarantees
jockeying Spanish national money away from the Vatican
in the summer of 1933.

Many of the drafts for New York Hospital
"Emergency Department One" protocols
were written at my dining room table...
a table I shared for many years
with Alvaro's grandnephew,
a fledgling dreamer, one in the founding
circle of "E.D. One," fledgling dream
blooming into official certifications and protocols.

The words "Futurity" and "Funereal"
share a common root base.
Both are words connecting us
to the concept of "Mortality."
What we are left with is the language of the gesture
and the ongoing, continuing creation of the world
and the artistic urge to memorialize it.

My resources are finite,
but my capacity for empathy is infinite.
Trauma, like acknowledgement
and understanding, radiates out like a lotus.

It can cause one to go backwards—
to create an indelible memory…
or a lasting trigger.

Charged with trauma and urgency,
i.e., via Exile, Natural Disaster, Family Crisis,
Grief. And though acknowledgement is key,
all lenses distort…

and in that is the fodder
of Misunderstanding, Understanding,
and Art. But after all, metaphor
is the realm, the hinge,
where both the rational and the irrational
can abide together.

DACA, exile, the uncertainties
or certainties that arise with sudden change.
In times of stress, besides drugs, cellular data,
furniture that converts to a coffin, tv,
and organized sports, where are we to turn
for Future, Nutrition, and Comfort?

How are sailor and scorpions to navigate
When they cannot find the stars?

Trace contagion (Infectious disease: bacteria
and viruses — influenza / polio / HIV /
Covid / Hate, symptomatic, asymptomatic.
Where contracted? Who knows.
Who cares?) is not always invisible.
does not just disappear.

Is microscopic. Relative visibility.

URGENT CARE - 2

My capacity for empathy is infinite
but my resources are finite.

Of course, I am also one of the lonely creatures
in the world who may never know peace.

I once watched someone I loved
staring into the well at the end of the world.
And shortly after that I fell in
with a youth haunted by a future.

Lasting affection lies everywhere,
eager to disavow the very feelings

that will come to consume it:

"I am here at the door. Open up.
I am here to watch the game,
away from the friends
who are not still alive."

We hold with tenacity to categories,
afraid that without them,
everything will vanish into chaos.

URGENT CARE - 3

Dilemma: Inconsolable,

a sense of roiling anguish at society's
intolerance;

                always living with the doubt
that the center will very likely not hold.

A pair of dancing fools.

Regretting moments of passion the next day.

Flies never give up.
They keep returning to the fray.

Collect seeds in a timely manner
and sow them in a protected way.
"Native seeds are like teenagers.
They love to be together."

No good deed goes unpunished.

I'm not sure how good I am
at allaying chaos.

For now, everything is holding together….
Though, I have my moments,
the night still goes by.
"Aye yai yai!"

I have shepherd order for a long time,
but the older I get…. The less I know….
and the less I'm prepared for any
creative maneuvering…. Knitting….
Maybe. Maybe beadwork.

"I GOTCHER BACK"

He found me. Tucked himself under my arm
one night and asked if I was a predator.
I said, "No, Baby I am a widower."

He shot back, "So am I!"

So, our amble together has been
pretty profound from the get-go.

His husband was murdered
one night in the playground
of a small town in Mississippi,
a simple marijuana purchase
gone bad.

So, his loss—to criminal violence—,
too, was sudden. We all
have a different story.

The two of us are perhaps
more like hyper-tender brothers,
very aware of what the other
is going through. We are happy
and easy in one another's company,
each watching the other
find his way back into some sort
of trust. A protective, kind,
and loyal port of calm

                              in a world
where neither is ready to imagine
much in. Neither window, nor mirror.
We just sort of live in the moment,
have each other's back.

CHAOS

For now, everything is holding together....
Though I admit, I have my moments of doubt
about the sustainability of what
I currently have patched together.

ENVOI

Tell me my voice is too loud.
That I should take my cues—
rather than from Texas bravado—more

from how a small thing
of the world survives.

Notes

Estoque: Dance With Death
Estoque – a rapier, in bullfighter used to kill the bull
Montera – a matador's black hat

Querencia
Querencia - Haunt, place of
Sol y sombra – sun and shade
Tendido - one of several tiers of seats at a bullring that are located above the ringside rows

Spleen
English translation of the epigraph:
"The devil's finest trick is to persuade you that he does not exist."

Hanging From A Roses Stem
Dedicated to Nicholas Sioutos, Alpha of the poem,
and Barbara Morris, Omega of the poem.

The rosé's song in the second stanza are lyrics from

Stephen Stills, "Love the One You're With."
English translation of the French:
… a unique flower in the world,
which does not exist
anywhere except on my planet….
— The Little Prince

Sampson At The Mill
The parenthetical quote in the fourth stanza, is taken from correspondence with fellow artist Sarah Best.

Herding Lawyers Is Like Herding Cats
It is a joke. well, sort of. After working with me for many months, my lead probate lawyer … asked for a poem with more joy. So, I changed the last line of this poem. I changed the word "they" in the last line to "all the little darlings."

Meditation: Point Of the Eyes
The work:

1. Trust that all art comes from direct observation.
   (Eyes, ears, heart, always opened to the past,
   the present, the future: hindsight, insight, foresight.)

2. Mind the hinge between the Abstract and the Concrete.
   (Mind it with Specificity. Avoid generalities at all cost.
   The leak energy and frequent lead to confusion.
   They do nothing for raising the relief of one's clarity.)

3. Work without ceasing. (Prolific writing.)

4. Train to be able to work in a received form.
    (Adaptable confidence.)

5. Rewriting. (The power of final form is in the ability
   to edit: eye, ear, love, and fire).

If one is striving for elegance, it is using
the very least to get the most out of it.

Concentrate on what is original (mature quality fashion
not glitzy trend).
"Origin" has do with what is old, enduring....it is not
simply what is new.
You are the authority.... the "author" of your expression.

Prose moves forward.
Verse turns back on itself, boustrophedon.
All poetry is praise: "the pleasure which we derive from

the representation of the present is due not only to the beauty with which it can be invested, but also to its essential quality of being present." - Baudelaire
Those words, that way.

Whazup * Intact * Fine And Dandy
"People are just as wonderful as sunsets …"
~Carl R. Rogers

Urgent Care
Civilized man knows of hardly any other way of understanding things. Everybody, everything, has to have its label, its number, certificate, registration, classification. What is not classified is irregular, unpredictable, and dangerous. Without passport, birth certificate, or membership in some nation, one's existence is not recognized. We suffer from the delusion that the entire universe is held in order by the categories of human thought, fearing that if we do not hold to them with the utmost tenacity, everything will vanish into chaos.
~Alan Watts (Book: The Wisdom of Insecurity)

The quote about teenagers: —Heather McCargo.

THANK YOU

In Memoriam: Joseph Fetler Maloff, Richard Howard, J.D. McClatchy, William Matthews, and Marie Ponsot.

Sidhant Sontakke, Nicholas Sioutas, Buck Hawes, Linwood Johnson, Italo Mariano Sanchez, Josh Jones, Matthew Guthrie, and Patrickat Carr.

Sven and Nate Davisson, Daniel W.K. Lee, Octavio R. Gonzalez, Antonio Addessi, Emanuel Xavier Berger, and Christian Lee.

Cynthia Hogue, Pam Uschuk, Andre Carter Brown, Andy Young, Vievee Francis, Michael Dinwiddie, Don Yorty, Ron Drummond, Peter Covino, Elaine Sexton, Terry Galloway, Carolyn Revercomb, Jody Johnson, Guadalupe Ruiz Fajardo, Paz Tarrio, Richard Newirth, Arlyn García-Pérez, Shelby Marne, Reece Borden, Mary Marek, Venancia Segura, and Stacy Pauly.

Sherri Adler, Eddy Collyns, Jill Fretchman, Catalina Cardenas, Francisco Latorre Mello, and Nick Bowers.

And to all those who have nurtured me in New York, Spain, Italy, Germany, England, Nepal, India, Mexico, and Texas.

Printed in the USA
CPSIA information can be obtained
at www.ICGtesting.com
LVHW021536030124
767834LV00070B/801

9 781608 642977